I found Arise and Go to be a great read to challenge me to open my eyes and to see how God can use me and our congregation all around us. What I love about this read is I know Ronald's heart and life of compassion and service and it is evident in Arise and Go. You will be encouraged and challenged to make a Kingdom difference every day.

In Christ,
Mark Westerfield,
Senior Pastor

Pastor Bell masterfully guided the reader into not just who God is, but also how He wants to be connected to every area of our lives by providing ample testimonies of how there is nothing in our lives too small or big for the Lord. After each chapter, you are left with not only more instruction but also with how to apply the information you have received into growing your relationship with God by walking by faith. You get to see real life encounters with how God is faithful, merciful, loving and always on time! Pastor Bell encourages, edifies and walks out the faith-walk of the Christian believer to give you what you need to grow your relationship with God.

Elyse Kelly

# ARISE AND GO

-

# SERVING THE LORD WITH GLADNESS

-

A Journey in Developing a Heart for Outreach

Dr. Ronald E. Bell II

Copyright © 2020 Dr. Ronald E. Bell II

ISBN 978-1-892664-14-3
EBOOK ISBN 978-1-892664-15-0

All rights reserved. No part of this publication may be reproduced, stored in a retrieval system, or transmitted in any form or by any means, electronic, mechanical, recording or otherwise, without the prior written permission of the author.

Scripture passages from The Holy Bible, Amplified Version (AMP) are accessible through Biblegateway.com and are used by permission.

Photos provided by Pip Start, Inc. are used with permission.

Published by Bell Missions Publishing, Austin, Texas.

REL012020 | REL012070 | REL030000
Library of Congress Control Number: 2020905869

Printed on acid-free paper.

Bell Missions, Inc. 2020
Third Edition

# DEDICATION

I dedicate this book to all of those who have led me, whom I have led, and whom I have been able to serve alongside. I also dedicate this work to my wife and children who have had to "share" me over the years. In addition, I want to thank those who were a part of editing and giving feedback on this work.

# CONTENTS

|   | | |
|---|---|---|
|   | Foreword | ix |
|   | Acknowledgements | xi |
|   | About the Book | xiii |
| 1 | On your feet | Pg 1 |
| 2 | Now | Pg 5 |
| 3 | Applaud God! | Pg 9 |
| 4 | Bring a gift | Pg 13 |
| 5 | Of laughter | Pg 19 |
| 6 | Sing yourselves | Pg 25 |
| 7 | Into His presence | Pg 31 |
| 8 | Know this | Pg 37 |
| 9 | God is God, and God, God | Pg 43 |
| 10 | He made us | Pg 49 |
| 11 | We didn't make Him | Pg 53 |
| 12 | We're His | Pg 59 |
| 13 | People | Pg 65 |
| 14 | His | Pg 71 |

| | | |
|---|---|---|
| 15 | Well-tended | Pg 75 |
| 16 | Sheep | Pg 79 |
| 17 | Enter with | Pg 83 |
| 18 | The password | Pg 89 |
| 19 | "Thank You" | Pg 95 |
| 20 | Make yourselves | Pg 101 |
| 21 | At home | Pg 107 |
| 22 | Talking | Pg 113 |
| 23 | Praise | Pg 119 |
| 24 | Thank Him | Pg 123 |
| 25 | Worship Him | Pg 129 |
| 26 | For God is | Pg 133 |
| 27 | Sheer beauty | Pg 139 |
| 28 | All generous | Pg 145 |
| 29 | In love | Pg 149 |
| 30 | Loyal | Pg 155 |
| 31 | Always and ever | Pg 159 |
| | About the Author | Pg 163 |

# FOREWORD

Psalm 100 The Message (MSG)
**A Thanksgiving Psalm 100**
**1-2** On your feet now—applaud God!
Bring a gift of laughter,
sing yourselves into his presence.
**3** Know this: God is God, and God, God.
He made us; we didn't make him.
We're his people, his well-tended sheep.
**4** Enter with the password: "Thank you!"
Make yourselves at home, talking praise.
Thank him. Worship him.
**5** For God is sheer beauty,
all-generous in love,
loyal always and ever.

**The Message (MSG)**
Copyright © 1993, 2002, 2018 by Eugene H. Peterson

In Psalm 100, the psalmist calls us to give thanks to God through our worship, our service, our knowledge, and our faith. First worship: we and the whole earth are called to shout joyfully to the Lord and come into his presence with singing, for he is the creator of the ends of the earth and the one who will sustain us by his love through all eternity. Second service: we are called to serve the Lord with gladness, this certainly includes our worship but also our work and mission: the two being inseparable as we are his people called to glorify him in all that we do. Third knowledge, we have a firm foundation for our worship and work as we know certainly that the Lord is God, he is our God who has called us by name and loves us as his own. And finally, faith: we can be assured of our faith because he is faithful and his covenant faithfulness to us and to generations is without end.

    Dr. Bell demonstrates how these themes of worship, outreach (service/missions), knowledge and faith work together in *Arise and Go.* Dr. John Piper famously proclaims, "missions exist because worship does not"; the converse is also true, missions and outreach exist where worship is present. This devotional based on Psalm 100 will focus your heart on the worship of God, which must overflow to others. The nature of worship is corporate and congregational: it involves community and spills over from individual hearts to neighbors, from family homes to neighborhoods, and from local churches to communities. My prayer is that through this book your heart may be moved to worship God, and then go with thankfulness to call others join in worshipping Him as well.

Reverend Chris Fisher, Austin, TX

# ACKNOWLEDGMENTS

I would like to acknowledge all the leaders and volunteers of Praise in the Park, PIP Impact, Master Builder, Young Life, Fellowship of Christian Athletes (FCA), and all the other outreach teams that I have been able to grow and learn with as God has led and continues to lead all of us in sharing His love with others. Also thanks to Dr. Tifani Blakes, Elyse Kelly, Bishop L.A. Wilkerson, Chris Fisher, Mark Westerfield, Camille Minor and Josiah Bell for reading, contributing and editing.

# PSALMS 100

1 On your feet now - applaud God!

2 Bring a gift of laughter, sing yourselves into His presence.

3 Know this: God is God, and God, God. He made us; we didn't make Him. We're His people, His well-tended sheep.

4 Enter with the password: "Thank you!" Make yourselves at home, talking praise. Thank Him. Worship Him.

5 For God is sheer beauty, all-generous in love, loyal always and ever.

# ABOUT THE BOOK

In Acts 9:6, after Saul's conversion to Paul, God told him to arise and go into the city. I believe that God is speaking those same words to all of us. Once we know Him, we are to "arise and go" for Him, to serve Him with Gladness (Psalm 100:2). In His Power and for His Glory. I pray this book encourages, ignites and helps you to develop a heart for outreach, and that you seek God for direction to take action. Each chapter title of this book is comprised from the words in Psalm 100.

# CHAPTER 1
# ON YOUR FEET

## Introduction

There may be many times in our lives when we are down and have problems getting back up. It might be from a situation we have caused or something that just happened to us. We may not be able to control the incident, but we do have control over our reaction. Time to get on our feet. There are times when we must decide to get up, pick up our bed and walk, and choose to give praise and thanks to the Lord. For He is good and His mercy lasts forever. We elect to pray with thanksgiving.

# God

No matter what your level of faith, commitment or submission to the Lord Jesus, choosing to praise God will bring us to our feet, and having the ability to get on our feet will give us more reason to praise God.

# Encouragement

I encourage you to seek how you can get on your feet and serve the Lord where God has you now. At work, school, neighborhood, gym, family, etc. Seek and find a way to serve Him by loving others and by serving others.

# Outward

For thirteen years God called me to lead an outreach ministry called Praise in the Park. Our heart, call and focus was to see God praised outside the four walls of the church. We endeavored to get various Christian denominations, ethnicities, communities, interest groups, businesses and education facilities to come together to serve a region by actively supporting students and families. This was the foundation that we "got up on our feet" and stood on. We committed one to five years in each city park community we served. It was not easy; it took a lot to get on our feet. We faced rejection, trials, and many challenges as we encouraged others to "get on their feet" and serve together. There is a heart and vision that God has for each community. Our focus needs to be on the fact that we do not fight against flesh and blood but against principalities and wickedness in high places. We went door to door praying for individuals and families. We provided yard services, afterschool programs in STEM (Science, Technology, Engineering, Math), sports, dance and other activities, plus alternative Christian Halloween events. As we served in these ways, we gradually saw change.

## Get Up and Out

In our city, there have been many outreach movements. I have had the blessed opportunity to serve with Love the Rock, Global Day of Prayer, National Day of Prayer, Rez Week, Hopefest, and others. God wants to use *you* to bring His glory to His city. Will you stand on your feet and say YES?

## Prayer

Lord, please use me for Your glory in my city. Let me not lean on my own understanding (Proverbs 3:6) regarding what it may or should look like or not look like. I love You Lord, and I want to serve You. Stir up the desire within me to have a heart for those in my city and for my city; to have Your heart. I want what You want. I surrender.

## Scripture

Then the Levites—Jeshua, Kadmiel, Bani, Hashabneiah, Sherebiah, Hodiah, Shebaniah, and Pethahiah—said, "Stand up and bless (praise, honor) the LORD your God from everlasting to everlasting. May Your glorious name be blessed and exalted above all blessing and praise."

NEHEMIAH 9:5

# CHAPTER 2
# NOW

## Introduction

When I was younger there was a candy called "Now and Later". We would call it "now/later". As children, we frequently wanted our candy now rather than later. In our society and generation, more and more of us are wanting more and more to have what we want now rather than later, whether it be our food, music, relationships, or anything else. Preparing now is wise; being ready to wait for the outcome is also wise.

# God

God calls us to serve Him now. Not to harden our hearts when He calls (Hebrews 4:7). The time is *now*. There is a now to abide in faith, hope and love (1 Corinthians 13:13). There was a now for Christ to be glorified (John 13:31). Not a waiting, a now.

# Encouragement

I encourage you to start now by asking God where and how you can serve Him. How you can impact our generation with the love of God. If you are already doing it, be encouraged and do not grow weary in well-doing, for in due season you will reap a reward.

# Outward

During our years of serving with Praise in the Park (PIP), we often needed to heed to the urgency to move and seek a particular neighborhood; a particular partner or funder. We had to often move *now*. There often seemed to be a constant waiting and then an immediate need to move *now*. There was once when there seemed to be rain coming the day PIP was scheduled. There were suggestions and thoughts of maybe canceling or waiting. However, we believed and trusted God's prompting in our hearts to make a decision right then and there to *now* move forward in faith, trusting what we were aware of in our spirits, yet doubted with our senses. In the thirteen years of having Praise in the Park during the spring months in central Texas (March and April), none of the outreaches were rained out or cancelled due to weather.

## Get Up and Out

Are you ready to follow and obey God now, immediately, fully and joyfully? Take a look with your heart. Are you ready? If not, why not? I encourage us to seek our hearts for what may be hindering us to get out and serve. Be honest, be willing to change and ask God to lead you in changing. Be ready to get up and go out.

## Prayer

Lord, please give me the courage and audacity to obey You now. I pray that I hear Your voice clearly, knowing that as I acknowledge You in all my ways that You will direct my paths. I claim the promise from Your Word that You are directing me as I continue to acknowledge You. Not my will, but Yours be done.

## Scripture

For He says, "At the acceptable time (the time of grace) I listened to you. And I helped you on the day of salvation." Behold, now is "the acceptable time," behold, now is "the day of salvation."

2 Corinthians 6:2

# CHAPTER 3
# APPLAUD GOD

## Introduction

We applaud many accolades in our lives: goals, touchdowns, great singing, graduations, great speeches, and so on. Some of us may applaud from an innate desire and response to what we are thinking or feeling; however, some of us may applaud due to others beginning and we join in. No matter what the reason, it is a part of our lives. When I was a teenager in a governor's school, we had a tradition of giving standing ovations to anyone who asked at any time. It was a great experience. It could be during a meal, hanging out in the park, or in a large auditorium. When someone asked, I enjoyed being a part of giving it, and when I asked, it was great to receive.

## God

God inhabits the praises of His people (Psalm 22:3). We bless Him from our applause and from our praise and worship of Him. However, I believe we need to bless Him more than He needs to be blessed. It is more blessed to give than to receive. When we give praise to God, it does something within us. Peace and joy enters; depression, despair, confusion, anger and frustration leave. For the spirit of heaviness, we are instructed to put on the garment of praise (Isaiah 61:3).

## Encouragement

I encourage you that no matter what you are going through, praise God, worship Him, thank Him, applaud Him. Bless Him with your words, your actions, your mind and your heart. Bless Him with all that is within you. Bless Him whether you are alone or with others.

## Outward

Year after year with Praise in the Park (PIP), we encouraged others to come together in parks all over our city to praise God, to worship Him, to applaud Him; through singing, dancing, and serving. While we applauded God, churches, groups, and individuals from various walks of life, places, theologies, and beliefs would come together in peace, with love and joy as we applauded God together. Connections were made, burdens were lifted. People's natural and spiritual needs were served.

## Get Up and Out

Go and look for opportunities to applaud God whether alone or with others. Both are needed. Be like a moth drawn to a flame as we are drawn to atmospheres where God is praised, glorified and applauded. Invite others to join you. Ask to join others. Bless Him…. Bless Him … Bless Him….

## Prayer

Lord, please allow our hearts to burn with an uncontrollable desire to bless You, to thank You, to applaud You. You are the air that I breathe; without You I am nothing. I need You. Fill me with You, the lover of my soul.

## Scripture

Great is the LORD, and highly to be praised, And His greatness is [so vast and profound as to be] unsearchable [incomprehensible to man].

PSALM 145:3

# CHAPTER 4
# BRING A GIFT

## Introduction

There is a game you may have played called the white elephant game. A group of people take turns selecting gifts with involuntary exchanges. At the end, some are happier than others. Gifts are enjoyable to receive. Some of use like surprise gifts; others of us, not so much. When we go to parties, we take gifts. We have traditions of giving gifts at Christmas, at weddings, house warmings, birthdays, coming into the presence of royalty and other instances. A gift is valuable; the way the gift is presented is as important as the gift. We often wrap them in extravagant paper, with ribbons and bows. Our attitude of how we present the gift is important, and the love we have for the receiver of the gift is also essential.

# God

When the wise men came to meet Jesus when He was born here on earth, they brought gifts of frankincense and myrrh. For God so loved the world that He *gave*. He gave us a precious gift of transformation, salvation and new life through Jesus Christ. As we applaud God, our heart is to have an attitude of bringing Him a gift of praise and the enjoyment of worshiping Him for who He is. He has given us both natural and spiritual gifts.

# Encouragement

Lord, help me see my life as a gift from You. Also, as a gift to others. I want to be a cheerful giver in all I do. As You freely gave life to me, I submit to Your will to use me as You will. You are the potter, I am the clay (Isaiah 64:8).

Dr. Ronald E. Bell II

# Outward

One aspect that made Praise in the Park (PIP) and similar outreaches special and impactful was the focus of young people bringing and sharing their gifts and talents as an act of worship to the Lord for others to join in and enjoy. Whether the gift was drama, singing, rapping, dancing or spoken word, all gifts were welcomed. Various ages, cultures, and expressions of the Christian faith were represented. Hispanic, Korean, African American, Caucasian, and others. Baptist, Presbyterian, non-denominational, and others. Those on stage were bringing and sharing their gifts not as unto man, but unto God (Colossians 3:23).

We also separated, recruited and placed team members according to their God given make-up, spiritual gifting and what brought them life. We had a team for prayer, stage/park, evangelism, booths/community service, children's activities, public relations, volunteers/greeters/hospitality and food, scheduling and administration. We each brought our gifts and brought Glory to God as a team. Team leaders and members also were from different churches and cultural groups. All other impactful similar outreaches had a division of teams based on gifting.

## Get Up and Out

Seek how God has gifted you and look for ways to use those gifts to bless, uplift and edify others. Look for ways to bless neighbors, your community, your place of work, your family and others God brings you in contact with. Look to see how you can give your gift of servitude and God's love to help a hurting world. As you use your gifts to bless others, it will bless you, bless them, bless others that are watching and most of all, bless our heavenly Father.

## Prayer

Lord, guide and direct me to where You want me for this season in my life. You are the Alpha and Omega (Revelation 1:8). My beginning and end. Before I was in my mother's womb, You knew me (Jeremiah 1:5). As I acknowledge You in all my ways, direct my paths (Proverbs 3:6). Lead me to the green pastures where You need me and to the gifts You have placed inside me (Psalm 23:2). I love You Lord. I want to feed Your sheep (John 21:17). Please continue to order my steps (Psalm 119:133).

Dr. Ronald E. Bell II

# <u>Scripture</u>

And [His gifts to the church were varied and] He Himself appointed some as apostles [special messengers, representatives], some as prophets [who speak a new message from God to the people], some as evangelists [who spread the good news of salvation], and some as pastors and teachers [to shepherd and guide and instruct], [and He did this] to fully equip *and* perfect the saints (God's people) for works of service, to build up the body of Christ [the church].

EPHESIANS 4:11-12

# CHAPTER 5
# OF LAUGHTER

## Introduction

Laughter is contagious. The laughter of a baby or child is precious and brings smiles, delight and laughter to us. Growing up I enjoyed comedies. Even now, I enjoy being in atmospheres that will encourage me to laugh. There have been those (even me at times) who try to not laugh or smile when we would rather be mad or upset. There are also games such as "If you love me." A game where you have one person say, "Honey if you love me, smile," and the person has to say, "Honey I love you, but I just can't smile." If they smile they lose; if they don't they win. This is especially fun with teenagers. There is also a version of a game called Moo where you face off with another person and "moo," trying to get the other to laugh first. There is a saying (which is not in the Bible) that if you want to make God laugh, tell Him your plans. This implies that God's plans, with His sovereignty, are so much larger and fuller than ours can ever be, which is true.

# God

In Genesis 26:8, laughter is shown as a husband and wife enjoying each other's company. When he had been there a long time, Abimelech king of the Philistines looked out of a window and saw Isaac laughing with Rebekah his wife. Of course, there are other ways in which God uses laughter; I would like to focus on the laughter of joy. The Bible says that laughter is medicine for our soul (Proverbs 17:22). In serving the Lord, there should be a joy that ignites the giving and the giving in turn ignites joy. As we give to God and His sheep ["if you love me, feed my sheep" (John 21:17)], let's be cheerful givers (2 Corinthians 9:7)-- givers to God, to ourselves, to others, and to what God loves.

Dr. Ronald E. Bell II

## Encouragement

I encourage you to challenge yourself to give more, then watch and receive the joy and laughter that comes in your life. Laughter is contagious and giving is contagious. Give yourself freedom and liberty to live, to give, and to laugh. Give at home, at work, at church, wherever you go: give of yourself and your laughter.

## Outward

With Praise in the Park (PIP), there was a great focus of joy *before* in preparing, *during* in executing and *after* in reflection. There were often three characteristics that others would mention about PIP: the organization, the peace and the joy. Those who served, served with joy. They desired to be a part of the regional outreach. One of the largest challenges, while at the same time one of the largest rewards, was praying, seeking and listening for which skills others had, then discovering how to develop them, and how they could be uniquely used in PIP to bless the region.

## Get Up and Out

As a next step; seek what truly and uniquely brings you joy. It could be singing, serving, building, cooking, speaking, or praying. Whatever it is, find a way to do it for and with others in your everyday life and in your community. If you don't know what those things are that bring you joy, think back to when you were in elementary school and what you enjoyed, or ask those in your life that know you best, such as parents, friends, etc. Also, most importantly, pray and ask God, the One who made you and first loved you (1 John 4:19).

## Prayer

Lord, guide me, lead me, speak to me. Make Your voice clear for me to hear the purpose You have for me to serve You and be who You called me to be during this season in my life. The purpose that will bring joy and laughter to You, to me and to others. I trust that You will lead me. Thank You Lord for Your guidance, Your grace and Your sovereignty.

Dr. Ronald E. Bell II

# <u>Scripture</u>

A happy heart is good medicine *and* a joyful mind causes healing, But a broken spirit dries up the bones.

Proverbs 17:22

# CHAPTER 6
# SING YOURSELVES

## Introduction

"Sing, sing a song, Sing out loud, Sing out strong, Sing of good things not bad, Sing of happy not sad." This song by Joe Raposo has been one of my favorite children's songs. It is a reminder to enjoy singing of good things. I also like the song "Singing in the rain, just singing in the rain"[1]; this song is a reminder that even when our

---

[1] Brown, Nacio Herb and Arthur Freed. "Singin' in the Rain." 1929.

circumstances may not be what we want, we still can choose to sing and enjoy. Music has the ability to intensify moods.

# God

God's word reminds us that we are to "speak to each other in psalms and hymns and spiritual songs, singing and making melody in your heart to the Lord" (Ephesians 5:19). "God inhabits the praises of His people" (Psalm 22:3). There is power and peace, direction and purpose, joy and healing in singing songs to and about the truth and greatness of our Lord. Singing also has the ability to lift our spirits.

# Encouragement

I encourage you that whatever your mood is, sing. However you feel, sing. No matter how you sound, sing. There have been countless times when my mood is bad, my thoughts are confusing, my situation seems unbearable, and my present reality feels overwhelming. When in those times I begin to sing songs of hope, joy and perseverance (either on my own, with a recording, or with others), God's presence fills me. There is peace in the midst of the storm. "Where God's spirit is, there is liberty" (2 Corinthians 3:17). Liberty to live, love, and laugh.

## <u>Outward</u>

Our focus was to have the atmosphere of Praise in the Park (PIP) to be singing songs of praise and worship to honor our Lord. We did, however, allow schools and groups other than churches and Christian/Gospel groups to minister. Schools and other non-Christian groups were invited to sing and play traditional hymns and songs that honored our nation's foundation on God. We began praying a year before the event, up until the event, and the day of the event. The atmosphere was that of joyful singing and uplifting our Lord. In the thirteen years of the event, there were no incidents of fights, discourse, or other conflicts. All was submitted to God's sovereignty as we uplifted His name. We experienced many that were drawn to Him by way of healings, deliverances, salvations and rededications.

## <u>Get Up and Out</u>

Look for and seek opportunities to sing hymns and spiritual songs to others and with others. Also, look for ways you can support outreaches of praise and worship, especially in places outside of churches and other places of worship. Support with your prayers, your time by volunteering, your finances, your resources (lending sound equipment, tables, etc.) and also with your advice, for there is safety in a multitude of counselors (Proverbs 11:14). The world needs the gift of worshiping the one true God. Some may not yet be aware. Some are sincerely seeking, yet have not found Christ thus far.

# Prayer

Lord, please give me the creativity and boldness to be active and vigilant in spreading Your Word, Your glory and Your presence through the region in which you have placed me. Give me freedom and help me to remove any barriers I have so that I may worship You openly and freely whenever Your Spirit prompts me, whether in the grocery store, in the car, at work, or wherever I am. Use me to usher in Your Spirit to bring liberty to me and those around me. Singing and humming, softly and loudly, short times and long periods of time. I submit my will to You. I submit to Your Spirit. Give me a new song to sing to You (Psalms 40:3).

Dr. Ronald E. Bell II

## Scripture

Sing to Him a new song; Play skillfully [on the strings] with a loud and joyful sound.

Psalm 33:3

# CHAPTER 7
# INTO HIS PRESENCE

## Introduction

When some people walk into a room, we may say they have a great presence. At times we may hear of the presence of a certain odor in a room or a certain spice in a dish. A person's presence can bring joy and comfort, sadness and pain, indifference and mediocrity or a plethora of other emotions. A baby in the arms of a loving parent can sense love and safety in the parent's presence. Being in the presence of someone who is extremely angry can bring unrest and discomfort. Presence is important and makes a difference.

# God

God is Omnipresent. He is everywhere all the time. Always was, always is and always will be (Revelation 1:8). His presence brings fullness of joy. He is also Omnipotent--all powerful. And He is Omniscient--all knowing. God cannot be contained (I Kings 8:27) and His glory fills (2 Chronicles 5:14).

# Encouragement

Just as God's presence matters in our lives, your presence matters in other's lives. You may feel like no one notices or cares about you. You may be thinking that your birth was a mistake or that your life does not matter. I believe that God has purpose for you. Your presence matters. God had a plan for you before you were in your mother's womb (Jeremiah 1:5). He has great plans for you, plans that matter! Keep choosing to believe God's truth about you, about your presence. Allow His presence and Spirit to bring you purpose, joy and liberty.

Dr. Ronald E. Bell II

# Outward

One focus we consistently had at Praise in the Park (PIP) was a desire to welcome and honor God's presence. In all we did in planning and in execution, God's presence was desired. The administration team prayed and sought His presence before planning; the leadership team sought and basked in His presence at retreats; we all enjoyed His presence at the event. There was a supernatural and divine strength, grace and joy that was present with us and within us. A day that should have wiped us out gave us energy. We enjoyed going out to eat afterwards. We had great sleep that night. There was a great feeling of fulfillment and satisfaction in serving in God's Kingdom and seeing a desire of God's and ours come to pass. Souls were blessed, people were brought closer to God; some committed to serve and live for Jesus as their Lord and Savior. Some were encouraged to know that others cared enough to come to their neighborhood and share their presence with them, even as we all enjoyed God's presence.

# Get Up and Out

Seek and find ways that you can share your presence with others. And even more so, seek ways to share God's presence with others. Get involved in the lives of others. Make time in your schedule. Be okay in being interrupted by others (yet with boundaries).

## Prayer

Lord, I thank You for Your presence in my life. I love You. Lord, allow me to be more aware of Your presence in my everyday life. I desire to sense Your presence in every conversation, while driving, when at work, when at home, during times of recreation, and while on vacation. Your presence is lovely and beautiful to me. As a bride seeking the presence of the bridegroom, I seek You, as You are the bridegroom and we, the church, are Your bride (Isaiah 61:10). I will seek You, the one my soul loves (Song of Solomon 3:2). In Your presence there is fullness of joy. Where Your Spirit is, there is liberty (2 Corinthians 3:17). Lord lead me into the freedom and fullness of Your joy (Psalms 16:11). I long to be in Your presence.

Dr. Ronald E. Bell II

# <u>Scripture</u>

You will show me the path of life; In Your presence is fullness of joy; In Your right hand there are pleasures forevermore.

Psalm 16:11

# CHAPTER 8
# KNOW THIS

## Introduction

There was a saying, "Knowing is half the battle" from GI Joe. It is important to seek and to value knowledge. Knowledge is said to be power. Learning should be valued. As humans, often the things we learn, we forget. Even for a test, we may only commit to learn material in a *short-term* way. We are not committed to learning the material for a lifetime, only for a moment.

# God

There is a difference between knowledge, understanding and intimate knowing. Having facts is good; understanding the facts is even better, for the Bible says that in all your getting, get understanding (Proverbs 4:7). Having the wisdom of how to use the understanding is best. However, there is a knowing that is on the order of Adam knowing Eve (Genesis 4:1). A knowing that is intimate and purposed. A knowing that is potent to produce. God knows us in an intimate way. God desires us to seek Him in that similar way of being still and knowing that He is God (Psalm 46:10).

# Encouragement

I encourage you to seek to know God. God says in His word to love the Lord God with all your heart, mind, soul, and strength, and to love your neighbor as yourself (Mark 12:30). To know God is to know love, for God is Love (1 John 4:8). It must first start with us towards God, then us towards us, then with us towards others. I encourage you to seek to know and love God, to know and love yourself, and to know and love others. Knowing God is the start.

## Outward

When we started Praise in the Park (PIP), the vision was to see Jesus be praised in parks in our region, nation and the world. Initially, I saw it as our team needed to get it done. I eventually realized that the vision was God's and the team was God's. Not just the team I knew, saw and worked with regularly, but many more around the world who were given a similar vision within the same few years. Some birthed through radio stations, some through churches, some through corporations, and some through grassroot efforts. It was a blessing to connect with other Praise in the Parks around the nation, to see Praise in the Parks birthed from our group and hear about others around the world. It was a very special season. Our God-called gift was to focus on students, families, and community reconciliation. When other opportunities arose to become involved in, we had to know what was part of our call and what was not. We did not always get it right initially; but eventually God's will was done and our will was submitted to His.

## Get Up and Out

Take time to honestly and earnestly seek to know God, His will, His presence. Spend time alone in a park, walking, with music, in stillness, in quietness with God. Ask Him to give you His heart for Him, for yourself, and for others. Seek creative ways He may lead you to serve others in your neighborhood, in your community, at your jobs, at your schools, and in your city. God has a heart and plan for your community and He has a part for you to play.

# Prayer

God, please give me a heart to seek You, to love You, to know You. To love You with all my heart, mind, soul and strength, and to love my neighbor as I love myself (Mark 12:30-31). I love You Lord. Also, give me a heart to love myself, to know myself. You made me in a wonderful way (Psalm 139:14); I want to see me as You see me. Give me a heart to know and love those in my life-spaces, those I interact with, those You bring across my path. Use me to bring Your redemption to my city, to my region, to my community.

Dr. Ronald E. Bell II

# <u>Scripture</u>

"Be still and know (recognize, understand) that I am God. I will be exalted among the nations! I will be exalted in the earth."

PSALM 46:10

# CHAPTER 9
# GOD IS GOD, AND GOD, GOD

## Introduction

Who is God? When people on the street were randomly asked "Who is God?" in several video interviews, many were not sure and some gave Him many names. Some say all gods are the same, some say there is no God. Also, we often hear the word *god* used in cursing, in text language (OMG), very casually out of frustration or feeling overwhelmed. There has been a saying and a song made popular by a German philosopher in the late 1800's, "god is dead." There have also been movies and a song that counters, such as "God's Not Dead". There are many diverse answers out there to the question of "Who is God?"

# God

Without God being the focus, we would labor in vain (Psalms 127:1). For God is the beginning and the end. He was, is, and evermore shall be. God is known as El Shaddai (Almighty) (Genesis 35:11), Elohim (God) (Genesis 1:1), and Adonai (Lord) (Genesis 18:31). He is our fortress (Psalm 18:12) and refuge (Psalm 46:1). He is strong and mighty in battle (Psalm 24:8).

# Encouragement

I encourage you that when good happens and blessings come, acknowledge God for them. When tough times and challenges come, trust God through it. He is who He says He is. He is the great I AM.

# Outward

With Praise in the Park (PIP), God was the focus. We focused on God being acknowledged and

God being glorified. Our heart was that we be instruments to promote and bring God's original vision of a community. Each year we would pray to find out which park and community to serve. We were in our first community for three years, on the grounds of a school for two years, and at our last community for five years. All of the other locations lasted one year. In our last community, our focus expanded to children's ministry in the city's housing authorities, Bible studies in neighborhood homes, house repairs and clean-up for the elderly, widows and single parents, alternative Christian Halloween events (PIP FIRE), Easter events, Christmas evangelistic events which included gift give-a-ways, and other outreaches. God was acknowledged, spiritual conversations occurred, and many committed their lives to follow Jesus Christ as Lord. God did it all.

We also shared God and His love openly and joyfully. There were occasions when our sharing was not initially welcomed, yet eventually even the most initially hostile was softened and calmed by our sharing of God's love. The screaming, tenseness, and anger subsided on a number of occasions.

## Get Up and Out

Reflect and seek for yourself who God is to you in your life. Then seek what His purpose is for you. Also, seek how He is leading and guiding you to share your gifts and talents to those in your community: either individually, with a partner or with many others. Seek and ask Him to use you, then let go and enjoy the journey of great challenge and even greater joy. Know and trust that He great plans for you (Jeremiah 29:11) and that His will for you is best.

## Prayer

Lord Jesus, I surrender my life plans and agendas to You. Lord, lead me, guide me, use me. You are my God; I am Your sheep (Psalm 100:3). Lead me to Your pre-ordained and pre-purposed green pastures and still waters (Psalm 23:2). I commit to follow You all the days of my life. Allow me to share You without shame and without hesitation and with boldness and conviction of who You are and all that You are. I know and believe You love me and I trust You to lead me on the marvelous journey You have for me. Thank You.

## Scripture

In all your ways know *and* acknowledge *and* recognize Him, And He will make your paths straight *and* smooth [removing obstacles that block your way].

Proverbs 3:6

# CHAPTER 10
# HE MADE US

## Introduction

When you look at certain products, they often have a tag or imprint that says, "Made in U.S.A." or "Made in China" or "Made in Taiwan." There are also paintings, buildings and clothing known for who made it. Name brand items usually cost more because of who made them, and the history of quality from the manufacturer.

## God

God made each of us for His purpose (Ephesians 1:11). He has a plan for us (Jeremiah 29:11). Just as the maker of an item makes the item more valuable, so does our Maker make us more valuable. God made us wonderfully (Psalm 139:14). God made us in His image (Genesis 1:27). When God made us, He said it was good (Genesis 1:31). We are most valuable for many reasons; however, the most significant one is because we were made by an almighty and loving God.

## Encouragement

Accept and believe that you are alive today on purpose, His purpose. No matter what has been said to you or about you, you are valuable. You matter just the way you are. Know that God has great plans for you to be whole, for you to reach others, for you to serve this generation (Acts 13:36). No matter how much or how many times someone tells you how valuable you are, you must choose to believe it for yourself. Believe it today.

# Outward

In the more than twenty years of outreach ministering (Praise in the Park ministries and others) and sharing God's love with others, the one observation that stands out to me the most is that of how many of us don't believe we are valuable. Due to circumstances, abuse, neglect, rough experiences and challenging life happenings, we lose sight of our value to God and our purpose. Our value and purpose are due to the fact that He made us; it is not solely from what we do. Congress for Christ and other street evangelism ministries speak life, which has been the most freeing to some of those who have endured many challenges. Jesus said that He has come to preach the captives free (Luke 4:18). We did drug-prevention school assemblies using the vehicles of dance, drama and music, followed by youth rallies at local churches, which ministered to many young people. Speaking life into the youth, listening to them, loving them and believing in them was very valuable. We planted, we watered, and God brought increase (1 Corinthians 3:6).

There was also another instance where the Master Builder Ministry was ministering at an apartment complex and one of the students "lit up" after we kept repeating week after week the Master Pledge that states, "We are made for greatness." He finally got it; he received it.

## Get Up and Out

Meditate on this question, "How much do I believe that God loves me fully just as I am?" Seek in God's Word and listen for His voice to hear how much He unconditionally loves you, how beautifully He sees you, and how fully He receives you and freely forgives you.

## Prayer

Lord, help me see me the way You see me: loved, desired, beautiful, and wonderful. I love You, Lord. I know You love me. Help me to receive Your unconditional love and to love myself unconditionally. I accept that You made me on purpose and that how You made me and when You made me are good.

## Scripture

"Worthy are You, our Lord and God, to receive the glory and the honor and the power; for You created all things, and because of Your will they exist, and were created and brought into being."

Revelation 4:11

# CHAPTER 11
# WE DIDN'T MAKE HIM

## Introduction

In our technical society we often get to call the shots and make the decisions on what we invent and produce; however, we are not given the same legal protection if we did not make it. Whether it is a patent, trademark or copyright; if we make it, we have ownership. If we did not make it, we do not have ownership. In fact, making claims and attempting to take control, without permission, of something that we did not create, falls into the illegal and immoral category. Even if I build or create a business, I get to choose whether I share it with someone or not, whether I get help or not, or even whether or not I accept offered assistance.

# God

God is so great and awesome that He was not made by anyone or anything. The Bible says that He was, is and forever more shall be (Revelation 1:8). He is the Alpha and Omega, the beginning and the end (Revelation 1:8). He is not a creation of man; we as man are His creation (Genesis 1:26). God questioned Job to remind him that He is God, by asking, "Where were you when I...?" (Job 38:4).

# Encouragement

It is good not to have the pressure and responsibility to know all. We can enjoy and rest in God who does. We focus on His daily bread (Matthew 6:11) and what He has for us today, for tomorrow has enough worries of its own (Matthew 6:34). We did not "put in order" or "bring about" (Greek word "asah") ourselves.

## Outward

Through the years of serving in citywide ministry outreach leadership teams (such as Praise in the Park Ministries and others), our leadership team had to continually remind each other of the fact that PIP belonged to God and that we were the stewards. God chose to share the experience with us and we accepted. The vision was His; our role was to trust Him for the direction and provision as we yielded ourselves to be the "hands and feet" and walk out doing the work on a daily basis. Initially it was difficult not to stress over the budget, recruiting team members, finding partners, selecting locations, deciding on worship bands, figuring out what to add and what to take away, and the list goes on. But then as we rested in Him, we more deeply accepted and realized that there is a way to work and be rested, pursue and be peaceful, and seek solutions and answers and not be anxious. We did not make Him, nor did we make PIP. PIP was God's vision to reach His people and to take on regions spiritually, to glorify His name, to be conduits for His love, to witness His deliverance in others, and to trust Him for the beginning and ending of each season in each community.

## Get Up and Out

Seek God's heart and vision for how He might want to use you in His ministry to the city in which He has placed you. Challenge yourself to see that you are a steward of all you have rather than the final owner. Seek also to enjoy this season of your life with its many challenges and ups and downs, keeping in perspective that there is an eternal season that we are forever on with our Lord.

## Prayer

Lord, help me to see my relationships, my finances, and my giftings as Yours over which You have given me stewardship. Help us to keep in mind that we did not make You, us, or our lives. You are the author and finisher of our faith (Hebrews 12:2). You keep us. Anything that You give me the strength and creativity to create is all from what You have already created. You are El Shaddai, The God Almighty (Isaiah 6:3).

Dr. Ronald E. Bell II

# Scripture

The earth is the LORD's, and the fullness of it, The world, and those who dwell in it.

Psalm 24:1

# CHAPTER 12
# WE'RE HIS

## Introduction

Ownership is a reality of our world. In our everyday lives we own homes, vehicles, clothing, electronic devices and many other items. We own pets with joy and pride. We say, "That is my cat," or someone might say, "Whose dog is this?" We answer with conviction, "That is my dog." When something is ours, our desire is to care for and take care of what we own. When we borrow something from someone, we acknowledge that it is not ours and we aim to take care of it better than the owner. There have been times when I have loaned my car to someone and I had to confidently feel that the person would take care of my car at least as well as I would, if not better. Ownership matters.

# <u>God</u>

God is the creator of all, and He is the owner of all. He lovingly cares for us. The Bible states that if an earthy father would care for his child, how much more would our heavenly Father care for us? (Matthew 7:11). God cares for us with His unconditional love, His Agape love. With His care comes provision and protection. This does not mean that undesirable or unfortunate circumstances will never be allowed to happen in our lives; however, it does mean that whatever is allowed, we can know that God cares and that He is always with us. And that we may not understand, but we can choose to trust that it will all work out to our good because we love Him and are called according to His purpose (Romans 8:28). We see that God acts out of unconditional love for us. He has an eternal purpose and desires our growth and maturity.

## Encouragement

With ownership also comes stewardship and covering. I encourage you to take ownership over all that is entrusted to you and all that you are involved in. If you are a part of a church, business, family, group or organization, then it is not *them*, but it is *us* and *we*. This also includes our marriages, our children and our communities. Take ownership for the state of your community, your marriage, and your children. Seek to be a great steward of all that God has entrusted to you.

## Outward

In serving with citywide ministry outreaches (Praise in the Park Ministries and others), a large part of our joy and strength from serving various neighborhoods and communities was knowing and accepting that we were His, the event was His, and the ministry was His. We had to trust multiple times in multiple ways that God would take care of what was His. We struggled with the sickness of team members, we prayed and trusted for suitable weather, we took on challenges as we sought approval from city officials, and trusted that people's lives would be changed in the process.

There also have been other outreaches, such as Love the Rock, where thousands from over forty churches in a suburb of a major metropolitan area gathered to claim the area for Christ, and actively care for it and take care of it.

## Get Up and Out

Seek to take action in the next few weeks, motivated from a heart that takes ownership for people, groups and organizations to which you are connected. Offer to assist or take care of a responsibility or task for which someone may struggle.

## Prayer

God, allow me to realize, see and receive your Lordship in my life, Your ownership. I choose to trust you for direction, provision and protection. I know You love me and want the best for me. Give me strength and zeal to be a faithful steward of all You have entrusted to me, my family, my community and my life.

## Scripture

For we are His workmanship [His own master work, a work of art], created in Christ Jesus [reborn from above—spiritually transformed, renewed, ready to be used] for good works, which God prepared [for us] beforehand [taking paths which He set], so that we would walk in them [living the good life which He prearranged and made ready for us].

EPHESIANS 2:10

# CHAPTER 13
# PEOPLE

## Introduction

Some people are "people persons"; they love people. I myself am *sometimes* a people person. When I am, I really am; and when I am not, I am *really* not. It takes a lot of grace and patience to deal with and enjoy all types of people. We have various moods, various personalities, various background experiences, various likes and dislikes, various gifts and talents, and various perspectives. And at the same time we are trying to live at peace with one another at home, at work, at the grocery store, in parking lots and in our communities. It reminds me of the Beatles song lyrics: "All the lonely people, Where do they all belong?"

# God

We are all people; however, God calls us His sheep. Jesus told one of His disciples that if they truly loved Him, that they would feed His sheep as well as His lambs (John 21:17). God so loved the world that He gave His one and only begotten son for us (John 3:16); to be reconciled back to Him (2 Corinthians 5:18). God loves us, His people, His creation. He loves us in our frailty, in our sin, in our doubts and confusion. He loves us to the extent that nothing is able to separate us from His love (Romans 8:38).

# Encouragement

No matter where you are with accepting and taking ownership and covering of your family, those that you lead in business and those in your community, keep in mind that any progress is progress. Although you might not have the full heart and desire now, you may be in a place where you *want* to have that heart and desire. Being aware and feeling that you might want more is a great Get Up and Out. God wants to use you to reach others for Him; submit and enjoy.

# Outward

While being a part of city-wide ministry outreaches (Praise in the Park Ministries and others), the success was greatest when we were gathered together in unity. The Bible states that there are commanded blessings when we are operating in God's space (Psalm 133:3); the anointing (power, grace, etc.) flows from the top down. As we value our staff (the servants) and those we are called to minister to (those who are served), success happens. The ministries that thrived focused on caring for their staff, such as enforcing sabbaticals, having retreats, praying for one another, spending time with each other outside of ministry, supporting events in each other's personal and family lives, fitting talent with task, being positive, and speaking the truth in love. When our team was tight and loving, those we were serving were loved from our overflow; we served God and worked together, loving each other with our frailties, faults and differences.

## Get Up and Out

If you are a part of a ministry outreach team, continue to serve. However, focus more on how you can share God's love with those you serve (those in leadership over you, your peers, and those that you lead). Enjoy sharing God's love with your team and then enjoy seeing how God multiplies that as you serve the ones He has called you to serve.

## Prayer

Lord, I pray that You give me Your heart for your people so that I would love them and serve them. I am Your vessel; use me and send me according to Your expressed purpose and design for me in this time of my life, in this generation.

Dr. Ronald E. Bell II

# Scripture

But we have this *precious* treasure [the good news about salvation] in [unworthy] earthen vessels [of human frailty], so that the grandeur *and* surpassing greatness of the power will be [shown to be] from God [His sufficiency] and not from ourselves.

2 CORINTHIANS 4:7

# CHAPTER 14
# HIS

## Introduction

There are many times when someone will say, "He gave me his word," or "We shook on it," or "We had a gentlemen's agreement." Our word makes a difference. As we keep our word or "watch over our word," we build character in ourselves and trust in us from others. Even when there is a situation that may arise where we are not able to do what we said or intended to do, there is still respect when the change is communicated, beforehand when possible, or even afterwards with an apology.

# God

God watches over His Word to perform it (Jeremiah 1:12). He is not a man that He can lie (Numbers 23:19). He can swear by no other (Hebrews 6:13). God spoke the universe into existence (Genesis 1). There are many instances in the Bible where people such as Mary would say "according to Your Word, Lord," and it was done (Luke 1:38). God has called us to share the gospel (His Word in His love) and He has given us His Holy Spirit to empower us to do so (John 14:26).

# Encouragement

I encourage you to trust, follow and believe what God is leading you to do in your life. You may have had (in the past, currently or in the future) a desire to serve others, improve their quality of living, or make a difference in your community in some other way. Be open and submit to the possibilities.

Dr. Ronald E. Bell II

## Outward

Focusing on God's Word was one of the primary objectives of Praise in the Park. Praise in the Park was broken up into twelve ministries, each of which had the scriptural foundation of God's Word to lead and guide us. Performer contacts (Psalm 150:6), booths (1 Corinthians 12:12), hospitality (Matthew 28:19), evangelism (Matthew 28:19), prayer (James 5:16), publicity (Romans 10:20 & Psalm 105:1), children's activities (Matthew 19:14), administration (Habakkuk 2:2,3), stage/park (1 Kings 9:3); all was based on God's Word. The scriptural foundation of God's Word guided our decisions; we had the faith and hope and saw God be God in great and mighty ways in communities.

## Get Up and Out

No matter where you are with giving and keeping your own word, make a commitment to make a change for the better today. And regarding God's Word, make a commitment to read it, know it, believe it, live it, and trust it. Make a commitment that in your life it will be "according to His Word."

## Prayer

Lord, I desire to be a person of my word, to value my word and discipline my tongue. Also, I want to learn to hear and to trust more of Your Word. Bring Your Word alive in my life. I want to hear Your voice and to know Your Word. I want to have your Word illuminate and direct my paths (Psalm 119:105) and to have the purpose You have for me come to pass.

## Scripture

Let my [mournful] cry come before You, O LORD; Give me understanding [the ability to learn and a teachable heart] according to Your word [of promise].

PSALM 119:169

# CHAPTER 15
# WELL-TENDED

## Introduction

We refer to gardens and sometimes people as being well-tended, well taken care of. The opposite of well-tended is tossed aside, unused, overlooked, or deserted. I like when my lawn is well-tended, however at times I am not as diligent to be consistent to make the time to keep our lawn well-tended. No matter how often I get to tend to my lawn, I always enjoy caring for, tending to and improving my lawn. I definitely enjoy the final product and feel good about the work I put into it.

## God

God tends us well. He provides for us. He cares for us. He clothes the flowers in the field and feeds the birds (Matthew 6:30). It is He who gives us breath. It is He that wakes us up in the morning (not our alarm clock, not the sun, not another person, not our pet). It is Him. He grooms us and tends us by maturing us, walking with us through trials, and by giving us human caregivers (placing it on the heart of others to feed, care and teach us when we are born). God tends us well.

## Encouragement

No matter what your upbringing was, whether you felt well-tended or taken care of by God or by others, God loves you. If you felt you were well cared for, continue by caring well for others in your household, family and community. If you did not feel like you were, become what you did not have and give what you have not received. Sow where you have not reaped, and trust God to restore years that were stolen and to heal your broken heart (Joel 2:25, Luke 4:18).

Dr. Ronald E. Bell II

## Outward

PIP Compassion Ministries took care of homes in a community we served for five years. We helped take care of homes for the elderly, single parents and the disabled. It took a great deal of work to care for the community, care for the people, care for their homes, and care for people's physical and natural needs. Because of our love for those to whom God had called us, we took the time, energy (emotional, physical, mental, and spiritual) to tend *well*. Throughout the days, weeks, months and years; we lovingly gave and served. We worked in their homes, in their hearts, in their yards, and connected them to needed services; we walked with them. As we served them, they tended to and served others (i.e. volunteering, leading Bible studies in their homes and in other ways). There was much work to be done in some homes from years of neglect: trash removal, organizing, painting, tree pruning, and other needed upgrades and repairs were made.

## Get Up and Out

Seek who you can care for and how you can increase your tending. That may be raising the level of care for those you currently care for. Also consider adding another person or two (or group or community) to care for and tend.

## Prayer

Lord, give me Your heart to care for others. May I love my neighbor as myself (Mark 12:31) as you continue to teach me to love You and to love myself. Give me the heart of the Samaritan who stopped to care for the wounded Jewish man (Luke 10:25-37). And give me the heart to care for my neighborhood, workplace and community. Use me to make an impact for You in this generation in the various areas of influence You have given me.

## Scripture

"Look at the birds of the air; they neither sow [seed] nor reap [the harvest] nor gather [the crops] into barns, and yet your heavenly Father keeps feeding them. Are you not worth much more than they? And who of you by worrying can add one hour to [the length of] his life?"

MATTHEW 6:26-27

# CHAPTER 16
# SHEEP

## Introduction

Sheep need security. Usually where there are sheep, there is a shepherd. A shepherd that protects with his staff; and a shepherd that feeds and cares for his flock. Sheep have wolves as predators, sheep tend to wander, and sheep need to be fed. One interesting fact I recently learned about sheep is that they respond and follow the voice of their shepherd. Sheep are in need of security from their shepherd.

## God

The Lord is our shepherd (Psalm 23:1). He is our strong tower, our refuge (Psalm 61:3), our hiding place (Psalm 32:7). Our Lord is mighty in battle (Psalm 24:8). God says not to touch His anointed. He says to do no harm to His prophets (Psalms 105:15 and 1 Chronicles 16:22). He says that vengeance is His (Romans 12:19). With Him being our shepherd, we are cared for and protected.

## Encouragement

If you are in a place where you are struggling with fear and with not feeling secure, I encourage you to read Psalm 91. As you read, be reminded that God is our protector. Also be ready to believe and trust what you are reading. Approach Psalm 91 with a commitment to read and accept with faith that God is God, His Word is true, and that He is our protector (Psalm 18:2).

## Outward

Ensuring security and protection at Praise in the Park (PIP) events were at times challenging.

Not in the sense that there were many threats, but in the sense of how to balance the natural with the spiritual, how to balance trusting God and not having any security versus having many armed security guards and police officers. We often were led (after prayer) to have one or two plain-clothed police officers. In the thirteen years of the event, by God's grace, there was not a need to have to use them. Having the presence and being prepared was good; however, trusting God for protecting, praying for His peace, and being wisely attentive during the event helped prevent anything that could have turned into an issue. The fire and police departments regularly began to have an area at the event that benefited and assisted in their relationship with the community and assisted us with a presence of natural protection if needed. In the end we learned to come to know that God provides the protection through others, and at times also provides the protection Himself, all on His own.

## Get Up and Out

Trust in the security of the Lord. Pray, seek and even ask others about ways within you that may be tainted with anxiety, unrest or fear. Ask God to take them away.

## Prayer

Lord, please help me to trust in the security of You. You are my Shepherd. I shall not want (Psalm 23:1). I want to more deeply entrust and enjoy my dependence on You. I want to trust and depend on Your hedge of protection (Job 1:10). Please, by the power of Your Holy Spirit, remove anxiety, unrest and fear in Jesus name. Thank You, Lord. I love You.

## Scripture

When He saw the crowds, He was moved with compassion and pity for them, because they were dispirited and distressed, like sheep without a shepherd.

MATTHEW 9:36

# CHAPTER 17
# ENTER WITH

## Introduction

How we enter something, whether it be a place, a position, a situation, a relationship or a season has great importance. How a bride enters the sanctuary on her wedding day shows grace and class. The mindset a young person has, when entering college, will set the tone for their college career. How we enter a ballroom or a boardroom can either turn heads and command attention or have little to no effect at all.

# God

The way Jesus entered this world in human flesh was humbly in a stable (Luke 2:7). However, His entrance when He returns is to be with power and glory (Luke 21:27). The Bible says that there is no place we can go from His presence (Psalm 139:7). His presence can go with you and give you rest (Exodus 33:14). In His presence there is fullness of joy (Psalm 16:11). God's presence has many benefits in our lives and in the lives of others. God's presence makes a huge difference for the better. Enter into His presence and embrace His presence in you.

# Encouragement

I encourage you seek who God has called You to be. Seek out the purpose He has for you, the expression of Him that He wants to express through you. There is a world that, at times, needs something as pure and simple as your presence, because God's presence will shine through you to comfort and bless others. People's lives need your entrance.

## Outward

There was a time when we were ministering with a youth missions organization (Real Life Communications) where it was obvious that our entrance made a difference. We would often present drug prevention school assemblies throughout the state using the medium of dance, drama and music, and then hold youth rallies at the end of the week at a local church. Once, as we were entering a school as we normally would, one of the students came and told us that they could not go into the gymnasium where the assembly would be held. They expressed that it was holy ground and due to the dark place that they were in spiritually, they could not go. We did not broadcast that we were Christians, we had not preached, we did not wear Christian T-shirts, and we had not made any references to God. Just the way we entered made a difference. Because of Who we were associated with, Who we spent time with, Who we were submitted to and Who we represented, we were known by the spiritual authority in which we walked.

## Get Up and Out

Can you sense where someone is spiritually? Can you tell if someone is walking with

Christ? If you confess Christ as Lord and Savior, would others be able to tell if you did not tell them? Wherever or whatever your spiritual walk is, ask yourself if what is on your outside matches what is on your inside and vice versa. Would your presence fill the atmosphere you enter with the fullness of what is within you? If so, keep doing what you are doing; if not, do not feel condemned, but ask yourself why not, see if you even care. If you do care, conviction should follow and change is on the way. If you do not care, it's time to do some real deep soul searching as to who you are, where you are going and who you were created to be. Be willing to share the God in you with others.

## Prayer

Lord, fill me with You to the point that I am fulfilled and others around me are fulfilled from the overflow of me in you. I want to soak and bask in Your presence. I love spending time with You and want to know You more and more. I love You, Lord. Use me to share Your love with a hurting world.

Dr. Ronald E. Bell II

## <u>Scripture</u>

So that the priests could not remain standing to minister because of the cloud; for the glory and brilliance of the L ORD filled the house of God.

2 CHRONICLES 5:14

# CHAPTER 18
# THE PASSWORD

## Introduction

I remember the television game show, *Password*, that I enjoyed. In our society there are many uses and needs for passwords. Some are for internet security and others are family passwords to alert children to who and what is safe. The passwords for the internet, websites, and online accounts become more complicated with requirements as the need for security rises due to the increased hacking attempts. What started as four characters went to six numerical characters, then with special characters and now eight and twelve-plus passwords that also need to be changed more and more often. Passwords are a growing part of our culture and lives.

# God

In 1 Corinthians, God states through the apostle Paul that many things can be done that are great, however without love, it has little to no profit. Without love, our speaking with tongues of men and angels can be as irritating as a clanging cymbal. Without love, even knowing all mysteries and moving mountains with our faith, we are nothing. Even if I give to the poor to be able to boast, I gain nothing (1 Corinthians 13:3). God has a password and it is *love*. His unconditional love. The type of love that hopes all things, endures all things, believes all things and bears all things. His love never fails. It quiets us (Zephaniah 3:17). It covers a multitude of sins (1 Peter 4:8), and it casts out all fear (1 John 4:18).

# Encouragement

As conviction (not condemnation) comes regarding loving God, yourself and others, have patience with yourself. God's love is patient and kind (1 Corinthians 13:4).

# Outward

Over twenty years ago, I was part of a street evangelism team. Weekly, we would walk through neighborhoods for hours at a time sharing the love of God and praying with residents. One day while our various teams were sharing how our conversations and ministry to the neighborhood were going, we got into a discussion that polarized us into two categories. When it came to how we were leading people to accept Jesus as Lord and Savior, one was to ask them if they knew where they would end up if they died today, heaven or hell. The other was to ask if they knew that God loved them and that there was forgiveness and freedom available for them in Jesus Christ. The first way tended to nudge people to accept Christ out of fear of going to hell, the other was encouraging them to receive God's love where heaven would be a byproduct. There were much richer and deeper conversations and prayer focused around God's love for them. We got to plant and water; God did, is and always will bring the increase (1 Corinthians 3:6). The password to their heart was *love*.

## Get Up and Out

In your conversations and in your heart, begin to take notice of your speech and attitudes towards others. Are we treating others differently because of how we view the person or community? Do we feel that we are above or below someone else? Do we feel or believe that some are unlovable or that we are unlovable? Ask God to change your heart about yourself and others, that you would see and love them (and you) as He does. Let's walk in His password of love.

## Prayer

Lord, fill me with Your love by the power of Your Holy Spirit (Romans 5:2-5). Help me to know and receive Your love, to love myself and to love others with Your unconditional Agape love. I choose to believe that Your love never fails (1 Corinthians 13:8).

## Scripture

For God so [greatly] loved and dearly prized the world, that He [even] gave His [One and] only begotten Son, so that whoever believes and trusts in Him [as Savior] shall not perish, but have eternal life.

JOHN 3:16

# CHAPTER 19
# "THANK YOU"

## Introduction

When learning another language, one of the first things you learn is how to say "Thank you": Gracias, Merci, Grazie, Arigato, Do Jeh; the list goes on. A thank you can put a smile on face of a family worker, co-worker, neighbor or store clerk. These two words show appreciation and respect for another's actions or thoughts. Thankfulness is a key ingredient to healthy relationships.

## God

We thank the Lord for being Who He is, for creating us and giving us others in the form of rich relationships. We are able to thank Him for what He has done, and we can thank Him as well for what He has promised He would do. We can thank Him for how He loved and loves us, for His care for us, for His provision, for His protection. The list of things is endless, infinite. And the joy we receive from focusing and thinking on thanking Him is just as endless.

## Encouragement

I encourage you to thank God more and more for any and every reason you can think of. Also, look for reasons to thank others. Look forward to being grateful. And when others thank you, receive it. Don't feel condemned if you are not where you want to be in this area; continue moving forward. Any progress is progress.

## Outward

There were many PIP Start ministry events (Praise in the Park, Master Builder, Galatia self-defense and Relationship Salsa for Life) where "thank-you's" were happening and were important on many levels. As a leadership team, we prayed and thanked God for what He had done for the ministry, for what He was doing and what He promised to do. As we would pray and ask for God's will to be done in our ministry and in our lives, we would thank Him in advance for bringing it to pass in the future in His way and in His time. We thanked our sponsors and partners; our sponsors and partners thanked us. We thanked those we were serving, and those whom we were called to serve thanked us. The more we looked, the more we could find for which to be thankful and give thanks. Of course, there were things happening in the ministry and in our lives that were not the way we would have liked them. Some were uncomfortable or just unwanted. However, we were able to decide to rejoice and be glad in the day that the Lord made (Psalm 118:24). We could decide to be thankful for what was happening for the good (Romans 8:28).

## Get Up and Out

Consider ending each day thinking of and writing down what you were thankful for during the day. Include what you are thankful for to God, to others and to self. End the day with a call, text or email to someone, thanking them for what they have done and who they are. Try to be as specific as possible as to why. And look for opportunities throughout the day to thank co-workers, service workers, parents, children, others and God.

## Prayer

Lord, I want to live a life of thankfulness and thanksgiving towards You and those You have placed in my life. Please forgive me for taking for granted blessings that have come directly from You and those that have come through others. I choose to renew my mind now to be grateful and thankful. I am thankful for all You have done, for all You are doing and all You will do. I am thankful for You being who You are; My Lord, My Savior, My Portion (Lamentations 3:24), My All.

Dr. Ronald E. Bell II

## <u>Scripture</u>

In unison when the trumpeters and singers were to make themselves heard with one voice praising and thanking the Lord, and when they raised their voices accompanied by the trumpets and cymbals and [other] instruments of music, and when they praised the Lord, saying, "For He is good, for His mercy and lovingkindness endure forever," then the house of the Lord was filled with a cloud.

2 CHRONICLES 5:13

# CHAPTER 20
# MAKE YOURSELVES

## Introduction

As people we enjoy the creativity of making things such as cakes, meals, paintings, and bookcases. However, when it comes to us, it can be more difficult to make ourselves do something. Especially if some of the things are ingrained in our habits or appetites. It can be hard to start exercising, start saying "thank you," stop smoking, stop being mean, etc.

# God

God wills in us to do His will (Philippians 2:13). Making ourselves submit to God, while resisting the devil, causes the devil to flee (James 4:7). Keeping pride out of our lives is our responsibility; we are to humble ourselves (James 4:10). As we submit to God and humble ourselves, the ability to be used as God's instrument to others becomes freer and more effective.

# Encouragement

If you are in a place in your life where it is very difficult to start things that you really have on your heart to start, or to stop things that you really desire to stop, be encouraged. Although there is "will power" and "self-discipline," there is also God who works in us to desire His will (Philippians 2:13). Ask for and be ready to receive God's grace (His supernatural power) to do what He has placed on your heart. For as we commit our ways to the Lord, He gives us the desires of our hearts-- He places the desire in our hearts and brings the desire to pass (Psalm 37:4).

Dr. Ronald E. Bell II

# <u>Outward</u>

I have spent years serving as a campus advisor and also as a Board of Directors member for Fellowship of Christian Athletes (FCA) and Young Life. During those years, one account comes to mind very clearly and impactfully. There was a student (I'll call her Mary for the sake of confidentiality) who was raised in the church. She was involved with FCA in middle school and wanted to be involved in a Christian organization in high school. During a Saturday tutoring session, I noticed her FCA t-shirt and began a conversation with her about her previous involvement. I then invited her to attend FCA and Young Life. She came occasionally during that semester. However, she had the opportunity to go to the FCA camp that summer. When she returned, she was changed. She stated that she now realized that serving the Lord and being a Christian was not about following rules (the way she had previously lived), but was instead a personal relationship with the Lord. She shared with other students, who were positively influenced by her. She then got involved in Young Life at the school. Mary began to bring more and more friends whose lives were also changed. Initially she was "making herself" follow rules; however, that changed to receiving God's love and enjoying a vibrant growing relationship with Him. God made the change in her life; she just had to receive and embrace the free gift of a personal relationship with Christ.

## Get Up and Out

Think through your life: in what things or places in your life are you trying to make yourself do something or make a change that is not working? Ask God to change your heart about the issue. Also, share your struggle with a good friend. Ask that friend to help hold you accountable in pursuing the change you desire that is on your heart. Then follow God's lead in making the change in you. Allow the changed you to serve and influence change in others.

## Prayer

Lord, I submit to You, and I am committed to resist the devil that has to flee (James 4:7). As I commit my works to You, I know that You will establish my plans (Proverbs 16:3). As I commit my ways to You and trust You, I know that You will do it (Psalm 37:5). I acknowledge that Your power is much more effective and powerful than my willpower. I trust You, Lord. Please do the work in me needed to fulfill the purpose You have for me in my life at this time, in this season.

Dr. Ronald E. Bell II

# <u>Scripture</u>

"For it is [not your strength, but it is] God who is effectively at work in you, both to will and to work [that is, strengthening, energizing, and creating in you the longing and the ability to fulfill your purpose] for His good pleasure."

PHILIPPIANS 2:13

# CHAPTER 21
# AT HOME

## Introduction

When I hear the phrase "at home" I think of the song "Consider Yourself" from the Broadway musical *Oliver!* There is a line in this song that says, "Consider yourself at home, consider yourself part of the furniture...." Home is a special place for us. There is a wonderful feeling of being "at home," being able to relax, be yourself and be comfortable. Our habits, belief systems, and self-images are developed and nurtured at home. Where a house may be a *place*, being at *home* is settling into a place.

# God

Unity in a house is important for it not to fall (Mark 3:25). God's sees our bodies as the temple (home) of the Holy Spirit. Home is important to God. We read that the apostle Paul said that a leader in the church is to have order in his/her home before leading in the church (1 Timothy 3:4). We get to decide for us and our house whom will we serve or what we will serve (Joshua 24:15). Having, getting and keeping our house/home (physically and spiritually) in order is of great importance (Isaiah 38:1).

# Encouragement

Get to know those in the homes around you. Get to know the people in the place where God has placed you to live. Be proactive to do your part to make your house, community and relationships "home".

Dr. Ronald E. Bell II

# Outward

During the time when a team and I were doing mission trips to northeastern Mexico, we spoke with and prayed for individuals and families in parks and on the street. However, the most effective and deep times of connecting, ministering and reaching others was when we were in their homes. Although the parks and the street were neutral ground, being in someone's home seemed to put them at more ease. Even though at times some would be hesitant to invite us into their homes (although most would). Offering us something cold to drink was a norm. While they offered to serve our natural need for natural food and drink, we were there to offer to serve their spiritual need for spiritual food and drink. The conversations were great, the prayer was great, and the added closeness that the residents received toward the Lord was great. Also, we saw their hope and peace increase. Just as it took trust for them to allow strangers into their homes, it took our trust in God to enter their homes and partake of the food that was offered. Even with allergies, we would pray ahead of time for protection, and we committed to partake of whatever was offered. We had to commit and settle in to make ourselves at home and to feel comfortable. The times of planting and seeding and being a part of the process of God bringing increase in His people and His Kingdom were amazing (1 Corinthians 3:7).

There was also an outreach ministry in our city that focused on knowing and praying for our neighbors. This was more of a stretch than when in Mexico. We committed to learn the names of our neighbors and pray for them. I personally stopped just pulling into my garage. I had the habit of using the automatic control to close the door as I pulled in. Instead, I began to go out into my driveway and say hello to any neighbors that might have been outside.

## Get Up and Out

Consider a neighbor you would visit and share meal or a simple hello. Go out of your comfort zone and begin to know the people that live around your home. Seek to make your places of community home. Do your part.

## Prayer

Lord, give me a heart to know and have Your heart for those that live around me. Give me a heart for the people around me whether at home or abroad. Here I am, send me (Isaiah 6:8).

Dr. Ronald E. Bell II

# <u>Scripture</u>

Then my people will live in a peaceful surrounding, And in secure dwellings and in undisturbed resting places.

ISAIAH 32:18

# CHAPTER 22
# TALKING

## Introduction

Walking through an airport, train station, or subway during rush hour, we hear lots of voices, lots of talking. Talking within us, talking with those to whom we are speaking with, as well as all the other conversations that are happening. At times we put on the TV, radio or our electronic devices just to hear someone's voice, to hear them talking. We call and webcast to talk and to hear others talk. Our talking can be used for good, bad or indifference. Daily, there is lots of talking going on around us.

## God

God enjoys speaking to us and He enjoys us speaking to Him. The Bible states that when we call, He answers (Jeremiah 33:3). He spoke to Samuel (I Samuel 3:11), Moses (Exodus 3:4), Mary via an angel (Luke 1:26-28), and many others in the Bible. He also still speaks and communicates to us. He asks that we do not harden our hearts when He speaks/talks to us (Hebrew 3:15).

## Encouragement

Feel comfortable and confident to be yourself as you speak and interact with others. Just as you would share about a favorite food, a good movie, a pet, a school you attended or a family member, share about your relationship with God in your own way. Be honest, be sincere, be you.

## Outward

During the time when PIP Start ministries had over 100 volunteers a year, we had one particular young lady that was a wonderful help.

Although we were a Christian Ministry, we did not limit our volunteers to only Christians. This young woman (whom we will call Beth for confidentiality) was of the Hindu faith. She was very intelligent, nice, committed, and helpful. One day while she was working with me on rewriting some of our Master Builder STEM (Science, Technology, Engineering, Math) educational outreach materials, I asked her what she knew about the Biblical character part of the lesson she was working on. Her engineering background gave her great insight into the academic side of the work; however, I felt led by God to ask at that time regarding the spiritual. She shared that she did go to a Catholic school as a young girl. So, I confirmed that she did know about Jesus; however, then I asked her did she know what happened after the cross. Her answer, which surprised me, was "no." I asked her if she would like to know. She said yes. So right then I shared about the death, burial, and resurrection of Jesus Christ and that it was because of God's love for us. I shared Romans 10:8, 9 and John 3:16. Her soul was eagerly absorbing all that I was saying. I asked if she believed. She said yes. Then I asked her if she would like me to lead her in a prayer to accept Christ as her Lord and Savior. She said yes. Right then we took a work break and prayed. Afterwards, she was content, lighter, and I could tell there was a difference in her. Within a couple of weeks, she had to move out of town due to her spouse receiving a promotion in his job. Just from talking, God used me to bring a soul into His Kingdom. As we acknowledge Him in all of our ways, He does direct our paths (Proverbs 3:6). It says to me that if we are willing to open our mouths and share about who God is, and how He loves us, God does the drawing. One may plant, another water, however God brings the increase (1 Corinthians 3:6). And as we lift up Jesus, He will draw all men unto Him.

## Get Up and Out

Make a conscious effort to be more aware of your conversations. What conversations are you having that are taking away from your purposed time, such as gossip, slander, arrogant pride arguments and fleshly debates? Or conversations that are adding to your purpose or someone else's by edifying others, listening to a heart express pain or joy, or speaking of God's goodness? There are also other types of conversations that may be good in general; but these are surface conversations and may or may not be leading to our growth in God. Make a commitment to acknowledge God in your conversation and enjoy Him directing what you say (Proverbs 3:6). Greet and talk with one another in hymns and spiritual songs (Ephesians 5:19). Make life, God and His purpose the center of your conversations.

## Prayer

Lord, please guide and lead my conversations. I desire to converse with You more often, and to speak of and about You to others. You are The Way, The Truth and The Life (John 14:6). I want You to be the center of all I do and the reason for all I do and say, doing all things to the glory of You (1 Corinthians 10:31). Use me in each day and in each interaction that I have with others.

## Scripture

So then, whether you eat or drink or whatever you do, do all to the glory of [our great] God.

1 CORINTHIANS 10:31

# CHAPTER 23
# PRAISE

## Introduction

In most of our everyday lives, when we think of praise we often think about telling a child how great they are, or telling an employee of a job well done, or giving good compliments towards a group or a person of fame. Often praise is lacking in our lives. It is something we enjoy receiving, however, and we all can improve in giving more of it.

## God

God is always worthy of our praise (2 Samuel 22:4). He inhabits our praise (Psalm 22:3). Praising God lifts us from the low places where we might have been to a fuller mental state, a lighter soul, and a more joyful heart. In the book of Revelation, God is praised continually—"to the One who sits on the throne" (Revelation 5:13). Jesus said that if we did not praise Him, the rocks would (Luke 19:40). God is meant to be praised and we are meant to praise Him.

## Encouragement

No matter where you are with praising God (with all praise) or praising others (with appropriate praise), be encouraged that you can start improving. Remember that any progress is progress! Begin praising others more and see how they and you are drawn closer to God.

## Outward

Praise in the Park was an atmosphere of Praise. We included praising the Lord in word and song during planning meetings. We included praising the Lord in word and song throughout the event. And we included praising the Lord in word and song at our celebrations. Within that atmosphere was liberty and peace. During the thirteen years of serving with Praise in the Park, lifelong friendships developed. The garment of praise (Isaiah 61:3) encouraged and led us to battle thoughts and states of depression. There were many who received peace just from entering the park we were in. Prayer (communication with God) was our foundation and praise was our pillar. We praised God for the process He had brought us through. We praised Him for the deliverance and change He was orchestrating in the present. And we praised Him for the promise and expectation of what He was about to do.

## Get Up and Out

Seek how you can give more praise and thanksgiving to those that God has placed in your life and those He brings you into contact with. Improve on receiving praise without pride and also without low self-esteem. Receive it with an outward "thank you" to them and an inward "thank you" to Him. And seek to find time and make time to praise God more often for all He is and all He does in our lives.

## Prayer

Lord, give me a heart to praise you in all that I do, to praise you with all that I am, to praise You wherever I go. I will bless You at all times. I desire and commit to have Your praises forever be in my heart (Psalm 34:1). Lord, You are great, You are awesome, You are my portion (Psalm 115:57 and Lamentations 3:24). Use me, use my life, and use all that I do as an instrument of praise to You.

## Scripture

I will bless the LORD at all times; His praise shall continually be in my mouth.

PSALM 34:1

# CHAPTER 24
# THANK HIM

## Introduction

    We are usually taught at a young age to be polite, to say please and thank you. Many of us fall into a natural habit of saying "thank-you" often, and we learn how to say thank you in many languages. There are many ways to say thank you, for many reasons, to many people. And there is One that we thank above all others.

# God

Of all the people, places and reasons we can say thank you to and thank you for, the most important is God. Jesus thanked God before He broke the bread and fed the thousands (Matthew 14:13-21 and Matthew 15:29-39). Jesus also gave thanks for the last supper (Matthew 26:26). In just such a way, we can follow His example and make it a habit and commitment to thank God for our food. It reminds us of where our food comes from and it speaks to others that we believe and give thanks to our God before we eat. We can come into His gates with thanksgiving (Psalms 100:4) as we thank Him for all of His wonderful works in our lives (Psalm 9:1). Even as we bring our cares, issues and requests to God with thanksgiving, God's peace will guard our hearts and minds in Christ, which will surpass all of our understanding (Philippians 4:6-7). In all that we do, whether in ourselves or our families, at work or in the grocery store, in the church or in the community, we can give thanks to God (Colossians 3:7) and remind others to do the same as we lead by example.

# Encouragement

I encourage you to turn your complaints into thanksgivings. If you complain often about your spouse, co-worker, family member or neighbor, thank God that you have a spouse, co-worker, family member or neighbor (that you are not alone); and ask Him to give you grace to thank them for what they *do* (as opposed to complaining about those things that they don't do).

## Outward

There are times when I am out eating and either myself or someone I am eating with will ask our server if there is anything we can pray for them for as we bless our food. Sometimes the person becomes uncomfortable and tries to rush away, other times the person may feel slightly confused and give a general answer, yet at times the person is genuinely moved and touched in his or her heart, and they begin to share. One of these times, a young woman began to openly share how she was struggling as a single mom and how she wanted to get back into fellowship with God and others in a local church assembly. She stayed as we prayed with her and for her. As we gave thanks to God for our meal, we also gave thanks for her and the work that He was doing in her heart and life. Thanking God honors God and blesses us and others.

## Get Up and Out

If you are not thanking God for your meals currently, I encourage you to begin to do so. Make the commitment a habit. It does not have to be loud, obnoxious or rude. You can simply bow your head and silently thank Him with your lips. Stop, slow down, and thank God in reverence for who He is and what He is doing in your life. Also, be open and ask God to lead you in inviting servers to share a need. Give thankfulness for what God has done, is doing and will do. Commit to make it a lifestyle with faith and joyful expectation.

## Prayer

Lord, I ask You to lead me to more opportunities to thank You with others. I want to thank You in every occasion (2 Corinthians 9:11). I want to always thank You for Your unfailing love and Your wonderful deeds (Psalm 107:8) and to thank You for others You have placed in my life (1 Corinthians 1:4). I choose right now to give thanks to You in all circumstances (1 Thessalonians 5:18), to turn my complaints, griping, and anxieties into petitions, and requests to You in thanksgiving. I look forward to and receive Your peace that will guard my heart and my mind (Philippians 4:6-7). In Jesus' Name.

Dr. Ronald E. Bell II

# <u>Scripture</u>

For all [these] things are for your sake, so that as [God's remarkable, undeserved] grace reaches to more and more people it may increase thanksgiving, to the glory of [our great] God.

2 Corinthians 4:15

# CHAPTER 25
# WORSHIP HIM

## Introduction

In our everyday world, there are many things, ideas and people who are worshiped. Some of us may worship our job, others of us may worship our money. Some will even worship ideals of utopia or human kindness. We also may fall into worshiping people in authority or those we highly respect. If it is something we totally depend on, have trust in and are consistently thinking about, it is worship. If we are reverencing ourselves unto that thing or person, if it is our central object of affection, it may be something or someone we worship. Sometimes we worship what we do not know (John 4:22).

# God

There is one True God to be worshiped (1 Corinthians 8:6). Part of Abraham's worship of God was to go out and sacrifice (Genesis 22:5). We know God to be the God of Abraham, Isaac and Jacob (Matthew 22:32). A God of generations, stability, and eternity. Our eternal life is based on knowing Him, the only true God (John 17:3). God desires us to also go out and share who He is, so that others can also know Him and make disciples (Matthew 28:16-20).

# Encouragement

You may feel as if your focus or worship needs adjusting. If so, receive the conviction and seek God to make the changes. Seek to have God be the center of your affections and thoughts. Just as Abraham went to worship God by obeying and being willing to sacrifice (Genesis 22:2), let's seek to also be willing to worship with sacrifice. Our worship belongs to Him and Him alone (Exodus 20:5).

Dr. Ronald E. Bell II

# Outward

One of the most exciting, open, and fulfilling worship experiences was with Rez Week. A week of being in the middle of a large university campus in the middle of a large city, leading worship to God, was amazing. There is a style of worship known as "harp and bowl" that is common with the various Houses of Prayers located throughout the world. Some wonderful worship times that I have had the privilege to be a part of include: beginning the new year in 2001 from 1 am- 2 am in the morning in worship, regularly praying in a house of prayer, and Rez Week. As students of different walks of faith, beliefs, past experiences and mindsets were walking along to classes or taking breaks, they heard the worship of God in song, whether a cappella or accompanied by guitar and other instruments. Some came into the tent for prayer; others admired the God-inspired art work and others enjoyed the God-focused conversations. Many seeds were planted and many more watered, asking God to bring the increase (1 Corinthians 3:6).

# Get Up and Out

Consciously pray and spiritually seek to have God be the center of Your thoughts. Desire and make changes in your habits, heart, and mind. Have Him be the largest thought in your head and the biggest thing happening in your life.

## Prayer

Lord, keep my heart towards You in worship (Psalm 99:9). I give my body and my life to You as a living sacrifice (Romans 12:1). I worship You, Lord. I say that You are worthy to receive glory, honor and power. You have created all things (Revelation 4:11). I am created by Your will; my being is in you and because of You (Revelation 4:11).

## Scripture

God is spirit [the Source of life, yet invisible to mankind], and those who worship Him must worship in spirit and truth.

JOHN 4:24

# CHAPTER 26
# FOR GOD IS

## Introduction

The statement "God is..." can be completed in various ways; some of those ways are dependent on our relationship with Him. Based on our experience with Him, knowledge of Him, and what we have heard about Him, there can be a variety of answers about who God is.

# God

God is a consuming fire and a jealous God (Deuteronomy 4:24). He is merciful (Deuteronomy 4:31); He is our refuge (Deuteronomy 33:27) and strength (Psalm 46:1-2). He is gracious and compassionate (2 Chronicles 30:9), our portion (Psalm 73:26) and our help (Psalm 54:4). He is our sun and shield (Psalm 84:11). He is love (1 John 4:8). He is faithful (1 Corinthians 10:13). Abraham got to know God as Jehovah Jireh (God is provider) based on His experience of God providing for him (Genesis 22:8). Moses knew Him as Jehovah Nissi (God is our banner) based on His experience with winning a battle when his arms were raised and losing when his arms were not lifted (Exodus 17:11). The Israelites experienced God as Jehovah Rapha (God is our healer) when they were not plagued with the same diseases as Egypt (Exodus 15:26). No matter what our experience is with Him, we can do nothing without Him (John 15:5).

# Encouragement

I encourage you, whatever you are going through, know that God is with you. Continue to have faith and believe that He will show Himself to you. The challenges and stresses of life can be used to know Him in a closer and more intimate way.

Including the stresses of lack, complacency and success.

# Outward

There was a time when talking with a co-worker about life led to the privilege of being used to be a part of their salvation experience. I met with this co-worker one day after work. She was not interested in going to church. She was not interested in the Christian "religion." She probably would have considered herself agnostic. As I was sharing my story, telling how I came to know God through tragedy and life experiences, she became more and more interested in what I was saying. In fact, not just what I was saying, but Who I was speaking about. During the conversation, I asked her if she would like me to pray with her to receive Jesus as her Lord and Savior; she said yes. So right then on her front porch, I was able to lead her in a prayer of confession of her need for forgiveness and trust in Christ. It was a great day. By me simply sharing who "God is" to me, another's life was changed for the better for eternity.

# Get Up and Out

Think about, rehearse, meditate, consider, and journal who God is to you. Be ready to share.

Just as you would share about who your spouse is, who your children are, who your parents are, or who your pet is, be ready to naturally share about who God is to you. Ask God for opportunities to share with others, and enjoy the many conversations He will lead and guide you to participate in.

## Prayer

Lord, I love You. Thank You for all the experiences in the past, present and future that allow me to know You more and more. I pray for the faith of my grandparents, my parents, my pastor, my minister, my priest to become my own. And as I continue to know You more intimately, give me the situations, the words, and the boldness to share who You are to others.

## Scripture

Therefore know [without any doubt] *and* understand that the LORD your God, He is God, the faithful God, who is keeping His covenant and His [steadfast] lovingkindness to a thousand generations with those who love Him and keep His commandments.

DEUTERONOMY 7:9

# CHAPTER 27
# SHEER BEAUTY

## Introduction

Beauty is said to be "skin deep" and also to be "in the eyes of the beholder." There are some things in this world that many would see and judge as beautiful, such as a sunset or sunrise, and others that only one or a few would deem as beautiful, such as some artwork (maybe from a young child). Often beauty is subjective.

## God

The Bible speaks of God being of great beauty (Zechariah 9:17). As we are created in His image, we are beautifully and wonderfully made (Psalm 139:14). We are His masterpieces and His workmanship (Ephesians 2:10). When He made us, He called it good (Genesis 2:10). He loves us (1 John 4:19). His focus is not on our outward appearance, but our hearts.

## Encouragement

I encourage you to receive God's love and love yourself as He loves you. To see yourself as being wonderfully made, as being a masterpiece, as good. Regardless of how we see ourselves, or what we have heard, or what we believe about ourselves, let's make God's word true in our lives and every man (including us) a liar (Romans 3:4). Let's not call bad what God calls good (Acts 10:15).

## Outward

I served for years on the Dawson McAllister Hopeline, a Christian-based call-in program for teens. Teens would call with many issues, from school bullying to contemplating suicide. The most frequent calls I received dealt with boyfriend/girlfriend issues, which included dealing with identity and self-image. There were many young men who did not feel worthy because of a dispute or breakup with a girlfriend. There were also many young women who felt unwanted, unloved and not beautiful due to conflict or a breakup with a boyfriend. In both cases, most of the time the opposite-gendered parent was distant, and/or they were not in a close relationship with a caring adult. There was no one to counter the lie and speak the truth in love to their child. Being a part of a team to minster to their needs, we only had to listen and then speak life back into them. At the end of those calls, young people were uplifted and encouraged. Even if they were not Christians, they were given hope. Some confessed and came to know the Lord before the end of a call. If they were confessing Christians, they were reminded of God's truth about them, and they were able to receive prayer to strengthen and uplift their soul and spirit. Both Christians and non-Christians were able to be drawn closer to the Lord. They had to be reminded of their beauty and worth.

## Get Up and Out

Look for and seek the beauty that God has bestowed in you and on you. He loves you. Also look for ways and opportunities to speak life into others by reminding them of their God-given beauty, both inside and out.

## Prayer

Lord, please give me Your perspective of the beauty You have placed in me and on me. I accept and receive Your view of me. I choose to agree with You that I am wonderfully made, a masterpiece. Made in Your image, I have value and I am beautiful.

Dr. Ronald E. Bell II

## <u>Scripture</u>

He has made everything and beautiful and appropriate in its time. He has also planted eternity [a sense of divine purpose] in the human heart [a mysterious longing which nothing under the sun can satisfy, except God]— yet man cannot find out (comprehend, grasp) what God has done (His overall plan) from the beginning to the end.

ECCLESIASTES 3:11

# CHAPTER 28
# ALL GENEROUS

## Introduction

Giving Tuesday, which was started in 2012, has become more and more popular. The Tuesday after Thanksgiving has become a focus on generosity. There have also been more occurrences of people opting to forgo gifts that would have been given to themselves and having that money raised on their behalf for a charity. Generosity is a part of our lives. It gives life to the giver and hope to the receiver.

## God

In the Bible, God conveys that a generous person will prosper. This is a matter of sowing and reaping (Galatians 6:7). As we refresh others, we also will be refreshed (Proverbs 11:25). God even promises to generously and liberally give wisdom to those of us who ask Him (James 1:5). God is generous, and He wants us to be generous.

## Encouragement

Stretch yourself to become more generous in your life. No matter where you currently are with generosity, consider becoming more generous. Our generosity blesses others and blesses us also; "It is more blessed to give than to receive" (Acts 20:35).

## Outward

There were many times during a five-year commitment to a local community where we gave gifts to those in low-income housing authority properties with PIP Impact. We freely gave to their natural need of food and toys for Christmas and freely gave of the gospel. Many were grateful and many were drawn closer to the Lord. There were those who gave their lives to the Lord and those who recommitted. We also were planting or watering seeds for God to later bring increase (1 Corinthians 3:6). We gave to the natural and spiritual needs of communities through Praise in the Park and Hopefest. These were times of great work, yet also times of great joy as we allowed the love God placed in our hearts to inspire us to give to others generously and unconditionally. (Romans 5:5 and 1 Corinthians 13).

## Get Up and Out

Look for ways to be generous to those you know and those you don't know. Give to those on the street who are asking for food or money; prepare with non-perishable foods you can give. Give to your spouse, children, parents, extended family, and co-workers, not based on what they have done, can do, or promise to do for you, but because God has given us the opportunity to be more like Him and be givers. "For God so loved the world that He gave..." (John 3:16).

## Prayer

Lord, please continue to pour Your love into my heart. I pray that I will fully receive it and that I will give out our Your Agape love, but not out of obligation or guilt. Instead, I pray that I will give cheerfully and purposefully (2 Corinthians 9:7). I want to give as You give, and I want to be more and more like You each and every day.

## Scripture

The generous man [is a source of blessing and] shall be prosperous and enriched, And he who waters will himself be watered [reaping the generosity he has sown].

Proverbs 11:25

# CHAPTER 29
# IN LOVE

## Introduction

The concept of being "in love" has always been prevalent and common. We often speak of and seek to be "in love" with someone or to have someone "in love" with us. We also frequently become "in love" with objects or entities that are dear to us such as a car or a job. There is also the concept of speaking and treating others in love, which unfortunately doesn't seem to be common in our everyday society.

# God

God is love (1 John 4:8). The Holy Spirit fills us with His love (Romans 5:5). Love is not created by us to use as we please, but it is His to use as He directs. He calls us to love Him with all of our heart, mind, soul and strength; and to love our neighbor as we love ourselves (Mark 12:30-31). His love allows us to love ourselves and others. His love believes all things, hopes all things, endures all things, bears all things; His love never fails (1 Corinthians 13:8). Many things in this world will fail, but God's love will never fail.

# Encouragement

I encourage you to be patient with yourself regarding loving God, yourself and others. God's love is patient and kind. Allow yourself time to grow at the pace God has set for you. Don't be mean to yourself when you fall short of your expectations or the expectations others have set for you. Be kind and patient. God is a forgiving God. Confess your sins and shortcomings to Him; He is faithful and just to forgive (1 John 1:9).

# Outward

There was an outreach ministry by the name of Congress for Christ, where a group of us would go to a very popular hangout place in Austin called $6^{th}$ street. On $6^{th}$ street, there were many bars and clubs, with people of all ages and walks of life, people with money as well as those who were homeless. The weekends had the most traffic. On a frequent basis, a group of us would go to a major corner in the middle of $6^{th}$ street and share with people that God loved them. We would offer to pray with them and be available to minister to their needs. Once there was a homeless gentleman who approached a couple of us asking for money. Normally I might have be resistant to even began a conversation with him; however, God led us to talk to him. We found out that he was hungry and had not eaten for some time. We offered to take him to a food truck to purchase food for him. After being hesitant, reluctant and slightly resistant, he agreed. He continued to ask us why we were buying him food and asking what he had to do for it. We kept telling him it was free for him and that we did it because God loved him. We prayed with him. He was moved and touched by the kindness done in love. We were also matured and filled with joy because we were used by God and got to see hope instilled in another.

## Get Up and Out

Reset your mindset and renew your mind regarding giving and receiving love (Romans 12:2). Look at it this way: God is the one who gives you His love to use as He pleases. We do not have the capacity within our own will to consistently and constantly give love unconditionally. The main job of your spouse, children, family or friends is not to love you (although they should); your main job is to love them. The love of God that we give to others may not be reciprocated back to us from them, but it will come from God through someone. As we give, it will be given back to us, pressed down, shaken together and running over shall men (others) pour into our bosom (Luke 6:38).

## Prayer

Lord, please fill me with Your Agape unconditional love. I want to love You more fully and receive Your love. I want to love myself more fully and be able to receive love from myself. I want to love others more fully and be able to receive their love. You made me worthy to receive Agape love and You empower me to be able to give it. I do not want to hinder Your love flowing to me or from me.

# Scripture

If I speak with the tongues of men and of angels, but have not love [for others growing out of God's love for me], then I have become only a noisy gong or a clanging cymbal [just an annoying distraction]. And if I have the gift of prophecy [and speak a new message from God to the people], and understand all mysteries, and [possess] all knowledge; and if I have all [sufficient] faith so that I can remove mountains, but do not have love [reaching out to others], I am nothing. If I give all my possessions to feed the poor, and if I surrender my body to be burned, but do not have love, it does me no good at all.

1 CORINTHIANS 13

# CHAPTER 30
# LOYAL

## Introduction

In many cultures loyalty is highly valued. The ability to commit allegiance to a person, group or entity has merit. The retail industry has many variations of loyalty programs. Rewards and other lures encourage and attempt to draw in our allegiance to their company. We may even feel good about hearing of how we are "a loyal customer." Mothers are loyal to children, sports teams are loyal to their teammates and their team, and spouses are loyal to each other. There is honor, strength and unity in loyalty.

## God

God is always loyal. He promises to never leave or forsake us (Hebrews 13:5 and Deuteronomy 31:6), whether we are right or wrong, near or prodigal, at peace with Him or not. There is nothing that can separate us from His love (Romans 8:38). He is our Alpha and Omega, our beginning and end.

## Encouragement

I encourage you to take a hard look at your loyalty to God and His purposes. Are you committed to serve Him, fellowship with other believers, and share His love with others you work with no matter how you feel, no matter how you have been treated, not matter what rewards you may or may not receive?

## Outward

I have noticed that in the various places where God has placed me to work in the past twenty-plus years, He has had plans for that place to be an outreach post for Him. I am sent and placed as an ambassador for Him, to represent Him. God uses us to encourage other Christian believers, to bring peace to the hearts of others, to subdue the anger of the atheist towards Him, to bring people together regularly for prayer, and to be a prayer warrior for wherever we are and whomever is present.

## Get Up and Out

Put *action* to Your loyalty to God and His "program." If you currently are not involved in any action, then start. If you are, then pray for confirmation that where you are is where you still should be. If God confirms it, continue to be loyal to God and where He has you right now with all your all. Be all in.

## Prayer

Lord, please give me a heart of loyalty to You, to Your will and Your desires. Being associated with You and committing to You may or may not bring me favor with men and I am okay with that; I trust You. I thank You for Your loyalty to me, that

You sent Your son to die on a cross for my sins, that I might be forgiven and reconciled back to You.

## Scripture

But Ruth said, "Do not urge me to leave you or to turn back from following you; for where you go, I will go, and where you lodge, I will lodge. Your people will be my people, and your God, my God. Where you die, I will die, and there I will be buried. May the Lord do the same to me [as He has done to you, and more also, if anything but death separates me from you."

RUTH 1:16-17

# CHAPTER 31
# ALWAYS AND EVER

## Introduction

Often when we are young and in love, we believe that our first loves will be forever. For a few this sometimes becomes the case; however, for most of us it is not. We sometimes wish our clothing, cars or material belongings would last forever. For some of us, we wish our teenage weight and physical fitness would last forever. In our natural world, all things have a beginning and an end. They are not forever.

## God

God Reigns forever and ever through all generations (Exodus 15:18, Revelation 11:15, and Psalm 146:10). His honor and glory will be forever (I Timothy 1:17).

## Encouragement

No matter where your thoughts, beliefs, habits or actions currently are regarding reaching those around you with God's love, start where you are with what He has given you and where He has placed you.

## Outward

As I have been a part of numerous communities and city-wide ministry outreaches for over the past twenty-plus years, there is often a challenge of planning details in the natural/temporal while keeping the focus on the eternal regarding the life, salvation and relationship of Christ with others.

We have spreadsheets, forms, organizational structure, and other formalities, yet God is the one who directs and guides. We plan in wisdom and follow God's leading. We would say that the Holy Spirit trumps wisdom. We prepare in planning, proceed in prayer, and prove in purpose. We allow Him to shepherd us to green pastures and still waters (Psalm 23:2), knowing that unless the Lord build it, we labor in vain (Psalm 127:1). We may make our plans, yet it is He who orders our steps (Proverbs 16:9). There have been many times our plans could have seemed and felt as if they were wasted, however, we continued to find out time after time that He often uses the planning to prepare us and uses the process to be for His will and purpose (Isaiah 46:10).

## Get Up and Out

Dream and make plans for how God may want to use you to reach your community and city. He has created you with a unique set of God-given talent. He has allowed and brought you through unique purposes to bring glory to His name. We become instruments in the Master Director's hands. We are ambassadors for Him wherever He sends us (2 Corinthians 5:20). Decide today to commit for now, for always, and forever to make a difference for the better in our communities and serve our generation (Acts 13:36). Be an impactor.

# Prayer

Lord, use me, send me. I am Yours to use as You please. I surrender my plan, will and desires to You. You are the one who has made me. You knew me before I was in my mother's womb (Jeremiah 1:5). Let Your will be done in my life (Matthew 6:10).

# Scripture

"I am the Alpha and the Omega [the Beginning and the End]," says the Lord God, "Who is [existing forever] and Who was [continually existing in the past] and Who is to come, the Almighty [the Omnipotent, the Ruler of all]."

REVELATION 1:8

# ABOUT THE AUTHOR

Dr. Ronald E. Bell II currently serves as a field engineer and most recently served as STEM teacher, department chair and instructional coach in a local school district. He serves as an associate pastor of Agape Christian Ministries, Young Life Board member and an adjunct engineering professor at Huston Tillotson University. Dr. Bell served as a Congressional Page for Congress, was selected as part of the Texas Society of Engineers 2001 Engineering Dream Team and is a certified Christian counselor. He has over 30 years of experience in STEM research and K-16 education. Dr. Bell is blessed by his wife and two children and enjoys music, dance, and sports. He especially values his personal relationship with Jesus Christ. Personal Statement: Acknowledge God in all your ways and He will direct your paths (Proverbs 3:6).

For comments or questions contact Dr. Bell at ronaldbellphd@gmail.com. Webpage: http://tinyurl.com/bellmissions.

www.ingramcontent.com/pod-product-compliance
Lightning Source LLC
Chambersburg PA
CBHW071622080526
44588CB00010B/1237